Mary's Testament

MARY'S TESTAMENT

OF THE NATIVITY AND THE DESTINY OF JOHN THE BAPTIST

Philip Robinson

ULSTER-SCOTS ACADEMY PRESS

First published by the Ulster-Scots Academy Press

All Biblical quotations in this book are from the American Standard Version of the Bible (ASV) which is in the public domain,

ISBN 978-1-9163758-8-8

Front cover illustration is *Mary and Elizabeth with Jesus and John the Baptist* (1825) by Johann Friedrich Overbeck.

Back cover image is *St. John the Baptist as a child* (1625) by Bartolome Esteban Murillo.

CONTENTS

PROLOGUE

AN INTERWOVEN STORY OF TWO BIRTHS; THE FORERUNNER AND THE MESSIAH

The *Gospel According to St Luke* is the only book in the Bible to give an account of the birth of John the Baptist. The details of it were apparently provided to Luke as a first-hand account by Mary, the mother of Jesus, and her narrative is intentionally (almost inextricably) interwoven with her account of the 'first Christmas' – the conception and birth of Jesus Christ.

But Luke, the author of this *Gospel* was not present himself for any of the events in the life of Jesus. Pointedly, Luke says in the opening verses that what he has recorded was information 'delivered' by those that 'from the beginning were eyewitnesses'. Luke was indeed a reporter, not a witness, for he was a Greek convert – a physician, a travelling helper and companion of the Apostle Paul on his missionary journeys around the Mediterranean. During these trips they visited Ephesus more than once (as recorded not only in Luke's other book in the New Testament, *The Acts of the Apostles*, but also in Paul's *Epistle to the Ephesians*}.

It was probably in Ephesus that Luke met Mary, for that is where the 'beloved disciple' John lived with her. The Apostle John (not to be confused with John the Baptist), was the disciple that Jesus had spoken to from the Cross, giving him future responsibility for the care of his mother:

> *"When Jesus therefore saw his mother, and the disciple standing by whom he loved, he saith unto his mother, Woman, behold thy son! Then saith he to the disciple, Behold thy mother! And from that hour the disciple took her unto his own home"* (John 19: 26-27).

The details Mary gives about the birth of John the Baptist seems deliberately interwoven with her account of the conception and birth of her own son, Jesus Christ. But these births were linked by something much more important than the kinship connection that existed between the two mothers, Mary and her 'cousin' Elisabeth.

Gabriel's Message from God was that Zacharias and Elisabeth would have a child in their old age that they were to call JOHN. This John would, according to Gabriel, go before the Lord *"... in the spirit and power of Elijah, to turn the hearts of the fathers to the children, and the disobedient to walk in the wisdom of the just; to make ready for the Lord a people prepared for him."* Six months later Gabriel proclaimed to Mary that her child, (to be called JESUS), conceived by the Holy Spirit, *"... shall be called the Son of the Most High: and the Lord God shall give unto him the throne of his father David."*

The narrative of these two connected visitations of the Angel Gabriel, first to Zacharias and then to Mary, signifies that the chronology of the two births was also significant; John being 6 months older than Jesus, for he was pre-ordained 'to prepare the way'.

A summary outline of the sequence of events in the opening chapter of Luke's *Gospel* illustrates the interwoven nature of the unfolding story told by Mary:

Luke 1: verses 1-4: Introduction by Luke

Luke 1: verses 5-25: **The Angel Gabriel visits Zacharias in the temple in Jerusalem and announces Elisabeth and Zacharias are to have a son, John.**

Luke 1: verses 26-35: The Angel Gabriel visits Mary in Nazareth and announces she is to have a son, Jesus.

Luke 1: verses 36-38: **The Angel Gabriel tells Mary of the son Zacharias and his wife Elisabeth are having.**

Luke 1: verses 39-45: **Mary visits her cousin Elisabeth in Judea**

Luke 1: verses 46-55: Mary's *'Magnificat'* proclaimed in Zacharias's house

Luke 1: verses 56-66: **Mary stays three months with Zacharias and Elisabeth until John is born and circumcised**

Luke 1: verses 67-79: **Zacharias's *'Benedictus'* proclaimed in his own house**

Luke 1: verse 80: **And John, "*grew, and waxed strong in spirit, and was in the deserts till the day of his shewing unto Israel*".**

The interwoven story of two births – those of John the Baptist and of Jesus of Nazareth – is a story that appears in the first chapter of Luke's *Gospel* as a single narrative, bound together by the visitation of the Angel Gabriel to two different homes, first in Judea, then six months later in Galilee. Of course the two lives interwoven were not of equal status. John the Baptist, born of an *earthly* father was to be the 'herald' of the Messianic King and to 'prepare the way' for him. But Jesus Christ, born of a *Heavenly* Father, was the child 'born to be King' in fulfilment of the 'Law and the Prophets'.

Two questions might be posed – why does Mary (and indeed the Biblical Record) 'combine' the stories of the birth of John the Baptist and Jesus Christ? And, secondly, why does God break the 400-year long 'silence' of his unfolding 'Word' in scripture with an announcement, in the Holy Place of the Temple, of the conception, birth and destiny of John the Baptist, rather than that of Jesus? The answers to these questions lie in the ultimate continuity of God's word between the Old and New Testaments, rather than in any perceived 'break' or 'silence'.

A 400-year 'silence' of God's Word is ended by the news of the forthcoming birth of John the Baptist

God's final word of the Old Testament in the book of *Malachi*, written about 400 BC by the last of the post-exile prophets, foresees the future Advent of Christ. But this arrival of the Messiah was not to occur unannounced, even after 400 years!

Through the prophet Malachi, God had declared:

*"Behold, **I will send my messenger, and he shall prepare the way before me**: and the* Lord, *whom ye seek, shall suddenly come to his temple, even the messenger of the covenant, whom ye desire, behold, he cometh, saith Jehovah of hosts"* (Malachi, 3:1).

Over the 400-year intertestamental period, this promise may have lost some of its immediate effect, but the last two verses of the last chapter of *Malachi* (and significantly the final verses of the entire Old Testament) are even clearer. God's *final words* in the Old Testament declare that the coming "Day of the Lord" will be preceded by a messenger and forerunner:

*"Behold, **I will send you Elijah the prophet before the coming of the great and terrible day of Jehovah come: And he shall turn***

the heart of the fathers to the children, and the heart of the children to their fathers" (Malachi, 4: 5-6).

If we then fast-forward 400 years to the appearance of the Angel Gabriel to Zacharias in the inner sanctum of the Temple, the connection is of overwhelming importance in the scheme of things:

"And there appeared unto him an angel of the Lord standing on the right side of the altar of incense. And Zacharias was troubled when he saw him, and fear fell upon him. But the angel said unto him, Fear not, Zacharias: for thy supplication is heard; and thy wife Elisabeth shall bear thee a son, and thou shalt call his name John. And thou shalt have joy and gladness; and many shall rejoice at his birth. For he shall be great in the sight of the Lord, and shall drink no wine nor strong drink; and he shall be filled with the Holy Spirit, even from his mother's womb. **And many of the children of Israel shall he turn unto the Lord their God. And he shall go before his face in the spirit and power of Elijah, to turn the hearts of the fathers to the children, and the disobedient to walk in the wisdom of the just; to make ready for the Lord a people prepared for him."** (Luke 1: 11-17).

Among all the prophesies of the Old Testament that were fulfilled in the first Advent of Jesus Christ, that of John the Baptist being sent by God as a 'type' of Elijah to 'prepare the way' is not a matter of interpretation, but one that is confirmed in the New Testament. When Jesus asked a crowd that had gone out into the wilderness to see John the Baptist, who did they think they were meeting? He answered himself, quoting *Malachi*: *"But what went ye out to see? A prophet? Yea, I say unto you, and **much more than a prophet. This is he, of whom it is written, Behold, I send my messenger before thy face, who shall prepare thy way before thee.**"* (Luke 7: 26-27)

Looking back over their overlapping ministries, the reason the narratives of the births of Jesus Christ and John the Baptist are inter-twined is quite simple. The purpose and ministry of John the Baptist's life was pre-ordained by God as an enabling provision for the ministry and purpose of his Beloved Son in exactly the way that the Angel Gabriel had announced.

FRAGMENT

THE ANGEL GABRIEL HERALDS THE BIRTH OF JOHN THE BAPTIST AS A PRELUDE TO THE ADVENT OF CHRIST

(Luke 1: 5-25)

5 There was in the days of Herod, king of Judaea, a certain priest named Zacharias, of the course of Abijah: and he had a wife of the daughters of Aaron, and her name was Elisabeth.

6 And they were both righteous before God, walking in all the commandments and ordinances of the Lord blameless.

7 And they had no child, because that Elisabeth was barren, and they both were now well stricken in years.

8 Now it came to pass, while he executed the priest's office before God in the order of his course,

9 according to the custom of the priest's office, his lot was to enter into the temple of the Lord and burn incense.

¹⁰ And the whole multitude of the people were praying without at the hour of incense.

¹¹ And there appeared unto him an angel of the Lord standing on the right side of the altar of incense.

¹² And Zacharias was troubled when he saw him, and fear fell upon him.

¹³ But the angel said unto him, Fear not, Zacharias: because thy supplication is heard; and thy wife Elisabeth shall bear thee a son, and thou shalt call his name John.

¹⁴ And thou shalt have joy and gladness; and many shall rejoice at his birth.

¹⁵ For he shall be great in the sight of the Lord, and he shall drink no wine nor strong drink; and he shall be filled with the Holy Spirit, even from his mother's womb.

¹⁶ And many of the children of Israel shall he turn unto the Lord their God.

¹⁷ And he shall go before his face in the spirit and power of Elijah, to turn the hearts of the fathers to the children, and the disobedient to walk in the wisdom of the just; to make ready for the Lord a people prepared for him.

18 And Zacharias said unto the angel, Whereby shall I know this? for I am an old man, and my wife well stricken in years.

19 And the angel answering said unto him, I am Gabriel, that stand in the presence of God; and I was sent to speak unto thee, and to shew thee these good tidings.

20 And, behold, thou shalt be silent, and not able to speak, until the day that these things shall come to pass, because thou believedst not my words, which shall be fulfilled in their season.

21 And the people were waiting for Zacharias, and they marvelled while he tarried in the temple.

22 And when he came out, he could not speak unto them: and they perceived that he had seen a vision in the temple: and he continued making signs unto them, and he remained dumb.

23 And it came to pass, that, when the days of his ministration were fulfilled, he departed unto his house.

24 And after these days Elisabeth his wife conceived, and she hid herself five months, saying,

25 Thus hath the Lord done unto me in the days wherein he looked upon me, to take away my reproach among men.

Chapter 1

Zacharias and Elisabeth, the Levite parents

"There was in the days of Herod, king of Judaea, a certain priest named Zacharias, of the course of Abijah: and he had a wife of the daughters of Aaron, and her name was Elisabeth. And they were both righteous before God, walking in all the commandments and ordinances of the Lord blameless. And they had no child, because that Elisabeth was barren, and they both were now well stricken in years." (Luke 1: 5-7)

Both Zacharias and his wife Elisabeth were Levites, that is, they belonged to the Israelite tribe descended from Levi, one of Jacob's 12 sons in his family that had settled in Egypt nearly 2000 years earlier. The Levites were the 'priestly' tribe, but none more so than the branch of the Levites who were descended from Aaron.

When the 12 Tribes of Israel eventually returned from Egypt during the 'Exodus' they had grown to a massive nation. On return to the Promised Land of Canaan, however, the Levites alone were assigned no share of the land, as they were to be free to fulfil priestly duties, supported in the tribal areas by each of them. Indeed Moses and his brother Aaron, that had led the Israelites out of Egypt, were themselves descended from Levi.

Going back to the birth of Moses in Egypt on the banks of the Nile, over 1500 years before Christ, we are told that his parents were both Levites, like the parents of John the Baptist, although unlike for him, the parents of Moses are not named:

> *"And there went a man of the house of Levi, and took to wife a daughter of Levi. And the woman conceived, and bare a son: and when she saw him that he was a goodly child, she hid him three months. And when she could not longer hide him, she took for him an ark of bulrushes, and daubed it with slime and with pitch, and put the child therein; and laid it in the flags by the river's brink"* (Exodus 2: 1-3).

Not only were Zacharias and Elisabeth Levites, but both were also descended from Aaron, the brother of Moses. Elisabeth is actually described as one of the *"daughters of Aaron"*, while Zacharias was *"of the course of Abia,"* a subdivision of the descendants of Aaron.

About 1000 BC, when King David was *"old and full of days"* and had *"made Solomon his son king over Israel"*, he gathered together all the priests and Levites in preparation for the building of the Temple at Jerusalem by Solomon. The Levites then numbered 38,000 men over the age of 30 (the minimum age for a priest), of which

10,000 were assigned hereditary roles by 'courses' or streams of families as porters, officers and judges, besides *"four thousand were porters; and four thousand praised the* LORD *with the instruments which I made, said David, to praise therewith"* (1 Chronicles 23: 5). The remaining 24,000 Levites were to *"wait on the sons of Aaron for the service of the house of the* LORD*"*.

But what of the sons of Aaron themselves? We don't know how many there were, however King David had the sons of Aaron divided by lot into 24 'orders' or family streams, each for the most important duties in the Temple, and to act as *"governors of the sanctuary, and governors of the house of God"* (1 Chronicles 24: 5).

Zacharias was 'of the course of Abijah', and this was one of the 24 orders that David had divided the 'sons of Aaron' into. In fact, when lots were drawn, the course of Abijah was the eighth:

> *"Now the first lot came forth to Jehoiarib, the second to Jedaiah, The third to Harim, the fourth to Seorim, The fifth to Malchijah, the sixth to Mijamin, The seventh to Hakkoz,* **the eighth to Abijah**, *The ninth to Jeshuah, the tenth to Shecaniah ..."* (1 Chronicles 24: 7-11).

Besides the prominent position Zacharias held in the Aaronic priesthood, we are told that both he and Elisabeth were *"righteous before God, walking in all the commandments and ordinances of the Lord blameless"* and that they *"had no child, because that Elisabeth was barren, and they both were now well stricken in years."*

Chapter 2

The priestly duties of Zacharias, alone in the 'House of Prayer'

"Now it came to pass, while he executed the priest's office before God in the order of his course, according to the custom of the priest's office, his lot was to enter into the temple of the Lord and burn incense. And the whole multitude of the people were praying without at the hour of incense. And there appeared unto him an angel of the Lord standing on the right side of the altar of incense." (Luke 1: 8-11)

The duty Zacharias was performing as a chief priest in the Temple at the time the Angel Gabriel appeared to him was occasioned by a unique set of circumstances which may have only occurred once in his lifetime. He had been chosen by lot among the men of the course of Abia, a small sub-group of the 'sons of Aaron', and his specific duty on this occasion was to burn incense on the Altar of Incense that was inside the windowless Holy Place of the House of the Lord. This Holy Place was inside the tabernacle building, out of sight of the 'multitude' in the temple courtyard, and contained the Altar of Incense and, to one side, the golden lampstand that burned continuously. The lamps on the lampstand also had to be tended twice daily, morning and evening by the designated priest.

The Altar of Incense stood just in front of the veil separating the Holy Place from the Holy of Holies – the inmost section that housed the Ark of the Covenant, topped by the golden 'mercy seat' between two golden cherubim. The Holy of Holies could only be entered through the curtain or veil by the High Priest once a year, to sprinkle blood from the sacrifice on the Day of Atonement.

In performing this particular duty of burning incense, Zacharias was also acting as Israel's intercessory priest for the prayers of the nation. This happened daily during temple worship involving praise (in Psalms), sacrifice and offerings (on the Brazen Altar), and the 'prayers of the multitude' in the courtyard of the temple.

The smoke from the Altar of Incense as the 'ascending prayers of the saints'

The Altar of Incense was inside the Temple 'House of the Lord' proper, while the Altar of Brazen Sacrifice was outside in the courtyard, in full view of the people who could assemble there for the twice-daily time of prayer. What Zacharias had to do was to place some burning coals from the Altar of Brazen Sacrifice onto a small fire-pan 'censer'. He then had to take the smoking censer inside the door of the Temple and sprinkle the incense powder on the burning embers, and place the whole on the Altar of Incense. This was to be done morning and evening at a time of public prayer.

The instructions for this Altar of Incense, its location, and the procedure for its use had been given by God to Moses:

> *"And thou shalt make an altar to burn incense upon: of acacia wood shalt thou make it. A cubit shall be the length thereof, and a cubit the breadth thereof; foursquare shall it be: and two cubits shall be the height thereof: the horns thereof shall be of one piece with it. And thou shalt overlay it with pure gold, the top thereof, and the sides thereof round about, and the horns thereof; and thou shalt make unto it a crown of gold round about. And two golden rings shalt thou make for it under the crown thereof, upon the two ribs thereof, upon the two sides of it shalt thou make them; and they shall be for places for staves wherewith to bear it. And thou shalt make the staves of acacia wood, and overlay them with gold. **And thou shalt put it before the veil that is by the ark of the testimony, before the mercy seat that is over the testimony, where I will meet with thee. And Aaron shall burn thereon***

sweet incense every morning: when he dress-eth the lamps, he shall burn it. And when Aaron lighteth the lamps at even, he shall burn it, a perpetual incense before Jehovah throughout your generations. Ye shall offer no strange incense thereon, nor burnt-offer-ing, nor meal-offering; and ye shall pour no drink offering thereon" (Exodus 30: 1-9).

As Zacharias was in the temple, *"the whole multitude of the people were praying without at the time of incense"*. The ascent of the sweet perfumed smoke from the Altar of Incense signified the prayers of God's people coming together before their God.

The incense

The recipe for the incense to be used in the temple included frankincense, and precise instructions for its preparation were given by God to Moses (Exodus 30: 34-38). It was 'Holy to the Lord', and anybody who violated this ban on its private or personal use was to be excommunicated from the congregation of Israel. The 'coals' from the perpetual fire on the Altar of Brazen Sacrifice were actually charcoal lumps specially provided and reserved for this use. Their burning represented God's righteousness, and the use of 'strange fire' from other sources on the Altar of Incense in worship was also strictly prohibited.

"And Nadab and Abihu, the sons of Aaron, took each of them his censer, and put fire therein, and put incense thereon, and offered strange fire before Jehovah, which he had not commanded them. And there came forth fire from before Jehovah, and devoured them, and they died before Jehovah. Then Moses said unto Aaron, This is it that Jehovah spake, saying, I will be sanctified in them that come nigh me, and before all the people I will be glorified. And Aaron held his peace" (Leviticus 10: 1-3).

Incense as Prayer

The ascending odour of incense from the Altar of Incense represented the prayers of the nation. King David prayed in Psalm 141: *"Lord, I cry unto thee: make haste unto me; give ear unto my voice, when I cry unto thee.* ***Let my prayer be set forth before thee as incense****; and the lifting up of my hands as the evening sacrifice,"* and the Apostle John's vision of heaven in *Revelation* 5 repeats the connection between prayer and incense: *"four and twenty elders fell down before the Lamb, having every one of them harps, and **golden vials full of odours, which are the prayers of saints.***"

Again in *Revelation* chapter 8 the smoke of the incense from the altar was associated with the prayers of the saints: *"And another angel came and stood at the altar, having **a golden censer; and** there was given unto him **much incense, that he should offer it with the prayers*** *of all saints upon the golden altar which was before the throne. And the smoke of the incense, which came with the prayers of the saints, ascended up before God out of the angel's hand."*

The Temple as the 'House of Prayer'

It is interesting that Jesus did not use the term 'temple' to describe the House of God. Rather, he alluded to the temple being his earthly body:

> *"Jesus answered and said unto them, Destroy this temple, and in three days I will raise it up. The Jews therefore said, Forty and six years was this temple in building, and wilt thou raise it up in three days?* **But he spake of the temple of his body"** (John 2: 19-21).

In contrast, when Jesus cast the moneylenders from the 'temple' he called it the 'House of Prayer'.

> *"And he entered into the temple, and began to cast out them that sold, and them that sold, saying unto them,* **It is written, And my house shall be a house of prayer:** *but ye have made it a den of robbers"* (Luke 19: 45-47).

Here, Jesus was quoting Isaiah in the Old Testament:

"Even them will I bring to my holy mountain, and make them joyful in my house of prayer: their burnt offerings and their sacrifices shall be accepted upon mine altar; **for mine house shall be called a house of prayer for all peoples***"* (Isaiah 56: 7).

The concept of the House of the Lord as a 'House of Prayer' rather than a 'Dwelling Place' containing God was emphatically reinforced by King Solomon when he opened the first temple building and prayed toward heaven before the Altar of the Lord:

"And Jehovah hath established his word that he spake, for I am risen up in the room of David my father, and sit on the throne of Israel, as Jehovah promised, and have **built the house for the name of Jehovah, the God of Israel***. And there have I set a place for the ark, wherein is the covenant of Jehovah, which he made with our fathers, when he brought them out of the land of Egypt.* **And Solomon stood before the altar of Jehovah in the presence of all the congregation of Israel, and spread forth his hands toward heaven***: And he said, O Jehovah the God of Israel, there is no God like thee, in heaven above, or on earth beneath, who*

keepest covenant and lovingkindness with thy servants that walk before thee with all their heart; who hast kept with thy servant David my father that which thou didst promise him: yea thou spakest with thy mouth, and hast ful-filled it with thy hand as it is this day. Now therefore O Jehovah, the God of Israel, keep with thy servant David my father that which thou hast promised him, saying, There shall not fail thee a man in my sight to sit on the throne of Israel, if only thy children take heed to their way, to walk before me as thou hast walked before me. Now therefore, O God of Israel, let thy word, I pray thee, be verified, which thou spakest unto thy servant David my father. **But will God in very deed dwell on the earth? behold, heaven and the heaven of heavens cannot contain thee; how much less this house that I have builded! Yet have thou respect unto the prayer of thy servant, and to his supplication, O Jehovah my God, to hearken unto the cry and to the prayer, which thy servant prayeth before thee this day; that thine eyes may be open toward this house night and day, even toward the place whereof thou hast said, My name shall be there: to hearken unto the prayer which thy servant shall pray toward this place:** *And hearken thou to the supplication of thy servant and of thy people Israel, when they shall pray* *toward this place: yea, hear thou in heaven thy dwelling-place; and thou hearest, forgive.*

…

What prayer and supplication soever be made by any man, or by all thy people Israel, *who shall know every man the plague of his own heart, and* **spread forth his hands toward this house: Then hear thou in heaven thy dwelling place, and forgive**, *and do, and render to every man according to all his ways, whose heart thou knowest; (for thou, even thou only, knowest the hearts of all the children of men)"* (I Kings 8: 20-30, 38-39).

The essence of the temple as a House of Prayer was that its use should conform *in obedience* to the precise forms of worship given by God, and *in humility* avoiding worship in 'self-will' that substitutes self-righteousness for the righteousness of God. So with Zacharias and Elisabeth, we are told at the beginning that they *"were both righteous before God, walking in all the commandments and ordinances of the Lord blameless."*

At this time, during the reign of Herod the Great in Judea (who was a vassal king of the pagan Roman Empire), even the High Priest and many of the ruling Jewish Council of Scribes and Pharisees were in closer communion with King Herod than with God. So, to have 'righteous' Zacharias ministering the incense of prayer was, in itself, something special.

From 'House of Prayer' to 'Den of Thieves' … and murderers!

Thirty years or so after the births of John the Baptist and Jesus Christ, the Gospels describe (apparently) two occasions on which Jesus entered the temple and 'purified' it by casting out the moneychangers. The first occasion was right at the start of his ministry, when Jesus first came to Jerusalem with his new disciples, and is described in John's *Gospel:*

> *"And the passover of the Jews was at hand, and Jesus went up to Jerusalem. And found in the temple those that sold oxen and sheep and doves, and the changers of money sitting: and he made a scourge of cords, and cast all out of the temple, both the sheep, and the oxen; and poured out the changers' money, and overthrew their tables; And to them that sold doves he said, Take these things hence;* **make not my Father's house a house of merchandise"** (John 2: 13-16).

On this occasion, before his 'rejection' as the Christ by the Jewish 'leaders' in Jerusalem, and when the 'Day of Vengeance of the Lord' would then, because of that, have to await a second coming or Advent, we do see a symbolic display of God's wrath in the driving out of the moneychangers with a whip. It was not an outburst of anger, for Jesus took the time to make 'a scourge of small cords' before overturning their tables. In this case he calls the temple 'my Father's house', but declaring that it had become a 'house of merchandise'.

Three years later, when Jesus enters Jerusalem again for the final time, the crowd are rejoicing and calling *"Hosanna! Blessed is he who comes in the name of the Lord, even the King of Israel!"* However, Jesus had earlier wept over Jerusalem because of his anticipated rejection, and we find a subtly different purification of the temple as he comes into the temple:

> *"And Jesus entered into the temple of God, and cast out all them that sold and bought in the temple, and overthrew the tables of the money-changers, and the seats of them that sold the doves; and he saith unto them, It is written,* ***My house shall be called a house of prayer; but ye make it a den of robbers"*** (Matthew 21: 12-13).

On this occasion no mention of a 'scourge' being used, but instead Jesus uses much harsher words. The 'House of Prayer' has been turned into a 'den of thieves'.

The other Zacharias, murdered at the Altar of Incense:

Of course, it was not only the moneylenders that had polluted the temple, but the very men responsible for religious leadership and temple worship. Jesus declared woe on them as well, and held them responsible for the generations of prophets and apostles that they had murdered and then built sepulchres for them. And so, *the blood of all the prophets, which was shed from the foundation of the world, may be required of this generation.*

"Woe unto you! for ye are as the tombs which appear not, and the men that walk over them know it not. And one of the lawyers answering saith unto him, Teacher, in saying this thou reproachest us also. And he said, Woe unto you lawyers also! for ye load men with burdens grievous to be borne, and ye yourselves touch not the burdens with one of your fingers. Woe unto you! for ye build the tombs of the prophets, and your fathers killed them. So ye are witnesses and consent of the works of your fathers: for they killed them, and ye build their tombs. Therefore also said the wisdom of God, I will send unto them prophets and apostles, and some of them they shall kill and persecute; **that the blood of all the prophets, which was shed from the foundation of the world,**

may be required of this generation; from the blood of Abel unto the blood of Zachariah who perished between the altar and the sanctuary: *yea, I say unto you, it shall be required of this generation*" (Luke 11: 44-51).

This is particularly interesting in that Jesus refers to *"the blood of Zachariah who perished between the altar and the sanctuary"* – in precisely the location that Zacharias (John the Baptist's father) was expected to emerge from the temple to address the 'multitude' praying outside and anxiously awaiting him.

The Old Testament account of the slaying that Jesus mentions – of another priest called Zacharias – refers to a time about 900 years B.C. when Joash was King of Judea. This Zacharias was stoned to death in the temple courtyard on the order of King Joash because he had condemned both the backslidden king and the people for their rebellion against God:

"And the Spirit of God came upon Zechariah the son of Jehoiada the priest, and he stood above the people, and said unto them, Thus saith God, Why transgress ye the commandments of Jehovah, so that ye cannot prosper? because ye have forsaken Jehovah, he hath also forsaken you. And they conspired against him, and stoned him with stones at the commandment of the king in the court of the house of Jehovah. Thus Joash the king remembered

not the kindness which Jehoiada his father had done to him, but slew his son. And when he died, he said, Jehovah look upon it, and require it" (II Chronicles 24: 20-22).

Jesus actually identifies where Zacharias was killed in the temple courtyard (between the altar and the temple), a detail not provided in the Old Testament account, except that he had 'stood above' the people in the temple court, perhaps on the temple entrance steps. (This temple was the first temple building constructed by Solomon).

Zacharias, thy prayer is heard!

When Zacharias was surprised by the appearance of the angel beside the Altar of Incense, the first words spoken to him were: *"Fear not, Zacharias, for thy prayer is heard."* The "whole multitude of the people were praying without at the time of incense," and the priestly duty Zacharias was performing was to delivery of the people's prayers to God in the prescribed form of worship.

Was the prayer of Zacharias that was heard, and answered, his personal prayer for a child, or his presentation of the multitude's prayer for deliverance of the nation of Israel? It is evident that it was both.

Chapter 3

The Birth of John the Baptist foretold by the Angel Gabriel

"And there appeared unto him an angel of the Lord standing on the right side of the altar of incense. And Zacharias was troubled when he saw him, and fear fell upon him. But the angel said unto him, Fear not, Zacharias: because thy supplication is heard; and thy wife Elisabeth shall bear thee a son, and thou shalt call his name John. And thou shalt have joy and gladness; and many shall rejoice at his birth. For he shall be great in the sight of the Lord, and he shall drink no wine nor strong drink; and he shall be filled with the Holy Spirit, even from his mother's womb. And many of the children of Israel shall he turn to the Lord their God. And he shall go before him in the spirit and power of Elijah, to turn the hearts of the fathers to the children, and the disobedient to walk in the wisdom of the just; to make ready for the Lord a people prepared for him." (Luke 1: 11-17).

The Angel Gabriel

The only person in the Bible that was addressed by an angel identified as GABRIEL *before* Zacharias, was the prophet Daniel in the Old Testament, during the Babylonian captivity (about 538 BC). It is intriguing to note that Daniel's vision happened when he was praying and 'presenting his supplication before the Lord', and that the message he was given was a prophesy foretelling the first Advent of Christ:

> "And **while I was speaking, and praying, and confessing my sin and the sin of my people Israel, and presenting my supplication be-fore Jehovah my God for the holy mountain of my God; Yea, while I was speaking in prayer, the man Gabriel, whom I had seen in the vision at the beginning, being caused to fly swiftly, touched me about the time of the evening oblation. And he instructed me, and talked with me, and said, O Daniel, I am now come forth to give thee wisdom and understanding.** At the beginning of thy supplications the commandment went forth, and I am come to tell thee; for thou art great-ly beloved: therefore consider the matter, and consider the vision. Seventy weeks are decreed upon thy people and upon thy holy city, to fin-ish the transgression, and to make an end of sins, and to make reconciliation for iniquity,

and to bring in everlasting righteousness, and to seal up the vision and prophecy, and to anoint the most holy" (Daniel 9: 20-24).

Only six months after the appearance of Gabriel to Zacharias, Gabriel appeared to Mary, as her testimony relates, to announce that she is to conceive Jesus 'of the Holy Spirit'. These three visions – of Daniel, Zacharias and Mary – are the only times an angel called 'Gabriel' is mentioned in the Bible.

What Gabriel says about the child Zacharias and Elisabeth will have

Gabriel told Zacharias that he and his wife Elisabeth would have a son; that he was to be called JOHN; and he will bring joy and rejoicing at his birth;

"For he shall be great in the sight of the Lord"

That this prophesy would be fulfilled to the letter became clear when the Lord Jesus declared to the people: *"Among those that are born of women there is not a greater prophet than John the Baptist"* (Luke 7: 28).

"And shall drink neither wine nor strong drink"

Jesus told the Pharisees *"For John the Baptist came neither eating bread nor drinking wine; and ye say, He hath a devil. The Son of man is come eating and drinking; and ye say, Behold a gluttonous man, and a winebibber, a friend of publicans and sinners!"* (Luke 7: 33-34). Indeed we are told that *"his meat was locusts and wild honey,"* so that in addition to not drinking wine, he also did not even eat bread!"

"He shall be filled with the Holy Spirit, even from his mother's womb"

Over six months later, we find fulfilment of this prophecy when Mary came to Zacharias's house having just conceived Jesus by the Holy Spirit: *"And it came to pass, when Elisabeth heard the salutation of Mary, the babe leaped in her womb; and Elisabeth was filled with the Holy Spirit: And she lifted up her voice with a loud cry, and said, Blessed art thou among women, and blessed is the fruit of thy womb. And whence is this to me, that the mother of my Lord should come unto me? For, behold, as soon as the voice of thy salutation came into mine ears, the babe leaped in my womb for joy."* (Luke 1: 41-44).

"He shall go before his face in the spirit and power of Elijah … to make ready for the Lord a people prepared for him"

With this final part of Gabriel's announcement, we move from details of John's future life as an individual to the announcement of the universal significance of his destined role as the prophesised 'forerunner' of the Messiah. In the prologue of this book, the Old Testament prophesies that John the Baptist was to fulfil are outlined – a messenger of God – Elijah the Prophet – to prepare the way before Him:

> "Behold, **I send my messenger, and he shall prepare the way before me**: and the Lord, whom ye seek, will suddenly come to his temple, and the messenger of the covenant, whom ye desire: behold, he cometh, saith Jehovah of hosts" (Malachi, 3:1).

> "Behold, **I will send you Elijah the prophet before the coming of the great and terrible day of the Lord: And he shall turn the heart of the fathers to the children, and the heart of the children to their fathers**" (Malachi, 4: 5-6).

The direct connection with this prophesy found in

Malachi was made in later years by Jesus Christ when speaking of John the Baptist:

> *"But what went ye out for to see? A prophet? Yea, I say unto you, and **much more than a prophet. This is he of whom it is written, Behold, I send my messenger before thy face, who shall prepare thy way before thee"*** (Luke 7: 26-27).

Zacharias is struck dumb by Gabriel

> *"And Zacharias said unto the angel, Whereby shall I know this? for I am an old man, and my wife well stricken in years. And the angel answering said unto him, I am Gabriel, that stand in the presence of God; and I was sent to speak unto thee, and to shew thee these good tidings. And, behold, thou shalt be silent and not able to speak, until the day that these things shall come to pass, because thou believedst not my words, which shall be fulfilled in their season. And the people were waiting for Zacharias, and marvelled while he tarried in the temple. And when he came out, he could not speak unto them: and they perceived that he had seen a vision in the temple: and he continued making signs unto them, and remained dumb"* (Luke 1: 18-22).

Clearly there were good reasons why the Baptist's father Zacharias was struck dumb by the Angel Gabriel until after the birth of John. Zacharias's role was not to proclaim the birth or the purpose of John's ministry to the waiting crowd in the temple, but to go home to his elderly wife and 'father' the child. Although the muting of Zacharias was seemingly given as a punitive measure by Gabriel, because of his lack of faith that an elderly and barren couple could possibly conceive a child, but the measure was full of purpose. Zacharias was not to suffer the same fate as his namesake who was stoned to death in the temple courtyard on the order of King Joash about 900 years before because he had condemned both the king and the people for their rebellion against God. Herod and the Pharisees would be condemned by John the Baptist himself, rather than by his father Zacharias. And John the Baptist would himself be put to death by King Herod, but not before his purpose was fulfilled.

Zacharias goes home to Elisabeth who then conceives his child

"And it came to pass, when the days of his ministration were fulfilled, he departed unto his house. And after these days his wife Elisabeth conceived, and she hid herself five months, saying, Thus hath the Lord done unto me in the days wherein he looked upon me, to take away my reproach among men.

Now in the sixth month the angel Gabriel was sent from God unto a city of Galilee, named Nazareth" (Luke 1: 23-26).

Zacharias was still unable to speak when he returned home from his term of priestly duties at the temple, and remained so until a week after the baby John was born. But in the sixth month of Elisabeth's pregnancy, the scene, and Mary's testimony, changes dramatically.

The angel Gabriel was sent from God when Elisabeth was six months pregnant to the northern town of Nazareth in Galilee.

Chapter 4

The Birth of Jesus foretold by the Angel Gabriel

"Now in the sixth month the angel Gabriel was sent from God unto a city of Galilee, named Nazareth, to a virgin betrothed to a man whose name was Joseph, of the house of David; and the virgin's name was Mary. And he came in unto her, and said, Hail, thou that art highly favored, the Lord is with thee: But she was greatly troubled at the saying, and cast in her mind what manner of salutation this might be. And the angel said unto her, Fear not, Mary: for thou hast found favor with God. And, behold, thou shalt conceive in thy womb, and bring forth a son, and shalt call his name JESUS. He shall be great, and shall be called the Son of the Most High: and the Lord God shall give unto him the throne of his father David: And he shall reign over the house of Jacob for ever; and of his kingdom there shall be no end. And Mary said unto the angel, How shall this be, seeing I know not a man? And the angel answered and said unto her, The Holy Spirit shall come upon thee, and the power of

*the Most High shall overshadow thee: where-
fore also the holy thing which is begotten shall
be called the Son of God"* (Luke 1: 26-31).

It is here that the familiar Nativity story starts in most people's minds, with no connection made to the birth of John the Baptist. But when Mary questioned how she could conceive as a virgin, Gabriel's response was not only to tell her that the child would be conceived of the Holy Spirit, but also that "with God nothing is impossible" for her cousin Elisabeth had conceived in her old age, and "this is the sixth month with her, who was called barren":

*"And behold, Elisabeth thy kinswoman, she
also hath conceived a son in her old age: and
this is the sixth month with her that was called
barren. For no word from God shall be void
of power. And Mary said, Behold the hand-
maid of the Lord; be it unto me according to
thy word. And the angel departed from her."*
(Luke 1: 35-37).

FRAGMENT

THE ANGEL GABRIEL HERALDS THE BIRTH OF JESUS, AND POINTS MARY TO ELISABETH'S HOME

(Luke 1: 30-56)

30 And the angel said unto her, Fear not, Mary: for thou hast found favor with God.

31 And, behold, thou shalt conceive in thy womb, and bring forth a son, and shalt call his name Jesus.

32 He shall be great, and shall be called the Son of the Most High: and the Lord God shall give unto him the throne of his father David:

33 And he shall reign over the house of Jacob for ever; and of his kingdom there shall be no end.

34 And Mary said unto the angel, How shall this be, seeing I know not a man?

35 And the angel answered and said unto her, The Holy Spirit shall come upon thee, and the power of the Most High shall overshadow thee: wherefore also

the holy thing which is begotten shall be called the Son of God.

³⁶ And behold, Elisabeth thy kinswoman, she also hath conceived a son in her old age: and this is the sixth month with her that was called barren.

³⁷ For no word from God shall be void of power.

³⁸ And Mary said, Behold the handmaid of the Lord; be it unto me according to thy word. And the angel departed from her.

³⁹ And Mary arose in those days, and went into the hill country with haste, into a city of Judah;

⁴⁰ And entered into the house of Zacharias, and saluted Elisabeth.

⁴¹ And it came to pass, when Elisabeth heard the salutation of Mary, the babe leaped in her womb; and Elisabeth was filled with the Holy Spirit:

⁴² And she lifted up her voice with a loud cry, and said, Blessed art thou among women, and blessed is the fruit of thy womb.

⁴³ And whence is this to me, that the mother of my Lord should come unto me?

⁴⁴ For behold, when the voice of thy salutation came

into mine ears, the babe leaped in my womb for joy.

45 And blessed is she that believed: for there shall be a fulfilment of the things which have been spoken to her from the Lord.

46 And Mary said, My soul doth magnify the Lord,

47 And my spirit hath rejoiced in God my Saviour.

48 For he hath looked upon the low estate of his hand-maid: For, behold, from henceforth all generations shall call me blessed.

49 For he that is mighty hath done to me great things; And holy is his name.

50 And his mercy is unto generations of them that fear him.

51 He hath showed strength with his arm; He hath scat-tered the proud in the imagination of their heart.

52 He hath put down princes from their thrones, And hath exalted them of low degree.

53 The hungry he hath filled with good things; And the rich he hath sent empty away.

54 He hath given help to Israel his servant, That he might remember mercy.

55 (As he spake unto our fathers) Toward Abraham and his seed for ever.

56 And Mary abode with her about three months, and returned unto her house.

Chapter 5

Mary travels to Judea to stay with Zacharias and Elisabeth

"And Mary arose in these days, and went into the hill country with haste, into a city of Judah; and entered into the house of Zacharias and saluted Elisabeth. And it came to pass, that, when Elisabeth heard the salutation of Mary, the babe leaped in her womb; and Elisabeth was filled with the Holy Spirit: And she lifted up her voice with a loud cry, and said, Blessed art thou among women, and blessed is the fruit of thy womb. And whence is this to me, that the mother of my Lord should come unto me? For, behold, when the voice of thy salutation came into mine ears, the babe leaped in my womb for joy. And blessed is she that believed: for there shall be a fulfilment of the things which have been spoken to her from the Lord" (Luke 1: 39-45).

For the first three months of Mary's pregnancy, she lived in the house of Zacharias and her cousin Elisabeth, until the time of John the Baptist's birth. Mary's arrival there was quite an occasion, for it involved an interesting affirmation that 'life' for unborn babies begins at conception. Mary was called by Elisabeth the "mother of my Lord", and her own babe "leaped in my womb for joy" when the voice of Mary's salutation "sounded in my ears."

Mary's response to Elisabeth was the familiar, prophetic "Song of Mary" known as the "Magnificat."

And Mary said, My soul doth magnify the Lord, And my spirit hath rejoiced in God my Saviour. For he hath looked upon the low estate of his handmaid: For behold, from henceforth all generations shall call me blessed. For he that is mighty hath done to me great things; and holy is his name. And his mercy is unto generations and generations on them that fear him. He hath showed strength with his arm; He hath scattered the proud in the imagination of their heart. He hath put down princes from their thrones, and hath exalted them of low degree. The hungry he hath filled with good things; And the rich he hath sent empty away. He hath given help to Israel his servant, That he might remember mercy; (As he spake unto our fathers) Toward Abraham, and his seed for ever. And Mary abode with her about three months, and returned unto her house" (Luke 1: 46-56).

FRAGMENT

THE BIRTH OF JOHN THE BAPTIST

(Luke 1: 57-80)

[57] Now Elisabeth's full time was fulfilled that she should be delivered; and she brought forth a son.

[58] And her neighbors and her kinsfolk heard that the Lord had magnified his mercy towards her; and they rejoiced with her.

[59] And it came to pass on the eighth day, that they came to circumcise the child; and they would have called him Zacharias, after the name of his father.

[60] And his mother answered and said, Not so; but he shall be called John.

[61] And they said unto her, There is none of thy kindred that is called by this name.

[62] And they made signs to his father, how he would have him called.

[63] And he asked for a writing tablet, and wrote, saying, His name is John. And they marvelled all.

[64] And his mouth was opened immediately, and his tongue loosed, and he spake, blessing God.

[65] And fear came on all that dwelt round about them: and all these sayings were noised abroad throughout all the hill country of Judaea.

[66] And all they that heard them laid them up in their heart, saying, What then shall this child be? For the hand of the Lord was with him.

[67] And his father Zacharias was filled with the Holy Spirit, and prophesied, saying,

[68] Blessed be the Lord, the God of Israel; for he hath visited and wrought redemption for his people,

[69] And hath raised up a horn of salvation for us in the house of his servant David

[70] (As he spake by the mouth of his holy prophets that have been from of old),

[71] Salvation from our enemies, and from the hand of all that hate us;

[72] To show mercy towards our fathers, And to remember his holy covenant;

[73] The oath which he sware unto Abraham our father,

⁷⁴ To grant unto us, that we being delivered out of the hand of our enemies should serve him without fear,

⁷⁵ In holiness and righteousness before him all our days.

⁷⁶ Yea and thou, child, shalt be called the prophet of the Most High: For thou shalt go before the face of the Lord to make ready his ways;

⁷⁷ To give knowledge of salvation unto his people in the remission of their sins,

⁷⁸ Because of the tender mercy of our God; whereby the dayspring from on high shall visit us,

⁷⁹ To shine upon them that sit in darkness and the shadow of death, to guide our feet into the way of peace.

⁸⁰ And the child grew, and waxed strong in spirit, and was in the deserts till the day of his showing unto Israel.

Chapter 6

John is born and the tongue of Zacharias is 'loosened'

"Now Elisabeth's full time was fulfilled that she should be delivered; and she brought forth a son. And her neighbors and her kinsfolk heard that the Lord had magnified his mercy towards her; and they rejoiced with her. And it came to pass on the eighth day, that they came to circumcise the child; and they would have called him Zacharias, after the name of his father. And his mother answered and said, Not so; but he shall be called John. And they said unto her, There is none of thy kindred that is called by this name. And they made signs to his father, how he would have him called. And he asked for a writing tablet, and wrote, saying, His name is John. And they marvelled all. And his mouth was opened immediately, and his tongue loosed, and he spake, blessing God. And fear came on all that dwelt round about them: and all these sayings were noised abroad throughout all the hill country of Judaea. And all they that heard them laid them up in their heart, saying, What then shall this child be? For the hand of the Lord was with him." (Luke 1: 59-66)

When Elisabeth gave birth to Zacharias's son, her neighbours and cousins 'rejoiced with her'. Their baby was a week old when it was due for circumcision, at which point his name was about to be recorded as 'Zacharias' after his father. But when Elisabeth declared that he was to be called 'John', and this was confirmed by Zacharias by writing on a tablet, their formal act of obedience to God and the angel Gabriel was rewarded. Zacharias's *"tongue loosed, and he spake, and praised God"*.

The words that Zacharias spoke when his tongue was loosed were no less than the prophetic "Song of Zacharias", known as the "Benedictus." In the first part of the Benedictus Zacharias declared with joy the fulfilment of God's promise of a Redeemer for Israel. This 'visitation' of the Lord to redeem 'his people' by raising up a 'horn of salvation for us in the house of his servant David' is a clear reference to the child Mary would have in six months. The second part of the Benedictus is a prophesy by Zacharias concerning his own son John, who would be 'called the prophet of the Highest: for thou shalt go before the face of the Lord to prepare his ways':

> *"And his father Zacharias was filled with the Holy Spirit, and prophesied, saying, Blessed be the Lord, the God of Israel; For he hath visited and wrought redemption for his people, And hath raised up a horn of salvation for us in the house of his servant David; (As he spake by the mouth of his holy prophets, that have been from of old), Salvation from our enemies, and*

from the hand of all that hate us; To show mercy towards our fathers, and to remember his holy covenant; The oath which he sware unto Abraham our father. To grant unto us that we being delivered out of the hand of our enemies should serve him without fear, in holiness and righteousness before him all our days. Yea, and thou, child, shalt be called the prophet of the Most High: For thou shalt go before the face of the Lord to make ready his ways; To give knowledge of salvation unto his people in the remission of their sins, because of the tender mercy of our God; Whereby the dayspring from on high shall visit us, To shine upon them that sit in darkness and the shadow of death; To guide our feet into the way of peace" (Luke 1: 67-79).

The Benedictus of Zacharias and the Magnificat of Mary together form a sort of 'dialogue' of complementary prophesies, even though they were delivered three months apart. Taken together they illustrate the harmony of Mary's testament as it describes the interwoven nature of the two births.

The child John – from his parent's home to the wilderness

There is even less information in the Bible about the early years of John the Baptist than there is about Jesus

Christ. With his parents being elderly at the time of his birth, it is unlikely they would have been still alive when he reached his boyhood years. Given John's fulsome knowledge of the Scriptures in his ministry, we may assume that he was instructed as a Levite 'son of Aaron' at least until the age of 12. But the implication of the last verse of *Luke*, chapter 1 is that John, while still a child, was living in the wilderness many years before his "shewing unto Israel" about the age of 30.

"And the child grew, and waxed strong in spirit, and was in the deserts till the day of his showing unto Israel" (Luke 1: 80).

Chapter 7

Mary and Joseph travel to Judea and Jesus is born

After the birth of John the Baptist, Mary had returned to Nazareth in Galilee, by which time she was just over three months pregnant. Her testament turns in *Luke* chapter 2 to the nativity of her own child, Jesus. It is remarkable to note that Mary is silent about the next six months in Galilee, and the narrative begins with the journey back to Judea where the story of the nativity of Jesus unfolds:

> *"Now it came to pass in those days, that there went out a decree from Caesar Augustus that all the world should be enrolled. This was the first enrolment made when Quirinius was governor of Syria. And all went to be enrol themselves, every one to his own city. And Joseph also went up from Galilee, out of the city of Nazareth, into Judaea, to the city of David, which is called Bethlehem, because he was of the house and family of David, to enrol himself with Mary who was betrothed to him, being great with child. And it came to pass, while they were there, the days were fulfilled that she should be delivered. And she brought forth her*

firstborn son, and she wrapped him in swaddling clothes, and laid him in a manger; because there was no room for them in the inn.

And there were shepherds in the same country abiding in the field, and keeping watch by night over their flock. And an angel of the Lord stood by them, and the glory of the Lord shone round about them: and they were sore afraid. And the angel said unto them, Be not afraid: for behold, I bring you good tidings of great joy, which shall be to all the people. For there is born to you this day in the city of David a Saviour, who is Christ the Lord. And this is the sign unto you; Ye shall find a babe wrapped in swaddling clothes, and lying in a manger. And suddenly there was with the angel a multitude of the heavenly host praising God, and saying, Glory to God in the highest, and on earth peace among men in whom he is well pleased. And it came to pass, when the angels went away from them into heaven, the shepherds said one to another, Let us now go even unto Bethlehem, and see this thing that is come to pass, which the Lord hath made known unto us. And they came with haste, and found both Mary and Joseph, and the babe lying in the manger. And when they saw it, they made known concerning the saying which was spoken to them about this child. And all that heard it wondered at *the things which were spoken unto them by the shepherds.*

But Mary kept all these sayings, pondering them in her heart. And the shepherds returned, glorifying and praising God for all the things that they had heard and seen, even as it was spoken unto them.

And when eight days were fulfilled for circumcising him, his name was called Jesus, which was so called by the angel before he was conceived in the womb. And when the days of their purification according to the law of Moses were fulfilled, they brought him up to Jerusalem, to present him to the Lord (as it is written in the law of the Lord, Every male that openeth the womb shall be called holy to the Lord), and to offer a sacrifice according to that which is said in the law of the Lord, A pair of turtledoves, or two young pigeons.

And, behold, there was a man in Jerusalem, whose name was Simeon; and this man was righteous and devout, looking for the consolation of Israel: and the Holy Spirit was upon him. And it had been revealed unto him by the Holy Spirit, that he should not see death, before he had seen the Lord's Christ. And he came in the Spirit into the temple: and when the parents brought in the child Jesus, that they might to do concerning him after the custom of the law, Then he received him into his arms, and blessed God, and said, Now lettest thou thy servant depart, Lord, according to thy word, in peace: For mine eyes have seen thy salvation, Which thou hast prepared before the face of all peoples; A light for revelation to the Gentiles, and the glory of thy people Israel.

And his father and his mother were marvelling at the things which were spoken concerning him; and Simeon blessed them, and said unto Mary his mother, Behold, this child is set for the falling and the rising again of many in Israel; and for a sign which is spoken against; yea, and a sword shall pierce through thy own soul, that thoughts out of many hearts may be revealed.

And there was one Anna, a prophetess, the daughter of Phanuel, of the tribe of Asher (she was of a great age, having lived with a husband seven years from her virginity; And she had been a widow even unto fourscore and four years), who departed not from the temple, worshipping with fastings and supplications night and day. And coming up at that very *hour she gave thanks unto God, and spake of him to all them that were looking for the redemption of Jerusalem.*

And when they had accomplished all things that were according to the law of the Lord, they returned into Galilee, to their own city Nazareth. And the child grew, and waxed strong, filled with wisdom: and the grace of God was upon him" (Luke 2: 1-40).

This is Mary's familiar story of the nativity of Jesus and these events are only recorded in this passage – the journey of Mary and Joseph from Nazareth to 'Royal David's City' (Bethlehem); no room at the inn; the birth of Jesus in a stable; laid in a manger; the angels appearing to the shepherds, and their visit of adoration.

After the birth of Jesus, the story continues with his circumcision a week later, and on the 40th day after his birth, the visit to the temple at Jerusalem to complete Mary's ritual purification after childbirth, and to perform the 'redemption of the firstborn son' by providing a sacrifice as required in the Law:

"Speak unto the children of Israel, saying, If a woman conceive seed, and bear a man-child: then she shall be unclean seven days; as in the days of her impurity of her sickness shall she be unclean. And in the eighth day the flesh of his foreskin shall be circumcised.

And she shall continue in the blood of her purifying three and thirty days; she shall touch no hallowed thing, nor come into the sanctuary, until the days of her purifying be fulfilled. But if she bear a maid-child, then she shall be unclean two weeks, as in her impurity: and she shall continue in the blood of her purifying threescore and six days. And when the days of her purifying are fulfilled, for a son, or for a daughter, she shall bring a lamb a year old for a burnt-offering, and a young pigeon, or a turtle-dove, for a sin-offering, unto the door of the tent of meeting, unto the priest: and he shall offer it before Jehovah, and make atonement for her; and she shall be cleansed from the fountain of her blood. This is the law for her that beareth, whether a male or a female. And if her means suffice not for a lamb, then she shall take two turtle-doves, or two young pigeons; the one for a burnt offering, and the other for a sin-offering: and the priest shall make atonement for her, and she shall be clean" (Leviticus 12: 1-8).

When Mary and Joseph brought the 5-6 week old Jesus into the temple at Jerusalem, it is very probable that Zacharias was there too. Indeed, given that Mary had stayed with Zacharias and Elisabeth for the first 3 months of her pregnancy, it seems likely that John the Baptist's parents were frequent visitors to Mary and

Joseph during the first weeks of Jesus's life.

Certainly, the occasion in the temple was in the public eye, for they encountered Simeon, who had been promised by God that he "should not see death, before he had seen the Lord's Christ." Simeon then took Jesus in his arms and made the prayer that is known as the 'Nunc Dimittis'; *"Lord, now lettest thou thy servant depart in peace, according to thy word: For mine eyes have seen thy salvation, Which thou hast prepared before the face of all people; A light to lighten the Gentiles, and the glory of thy people Israel."* Then Simeon prophesied; *"Behold, this child is set for the falling and the rising of many in Israel; and for a sign which is spoken against; yea and a sword shall pierce through thy own soul; that the thoughts out of many hearts may be revealed."* (Luke 2: 34-35)

An 84-year-old prophetess called Anna of the tribe of Asher was also in the temple. In fact she was constantly there, fasting and praying day and night. On seeing Jesus, Anna praised God and proclaimed to all that around this was the one they were waiting for who would redeem Israel.

Chapter 8

Jesus and John – the silent years of childhood

With one notable exception, Mary's testament of the nativity of Jesus tells us nothing of the flight to Egypt[1] or the later childhood years of her son after he was about six weeks old, simply stating: *"And when they had performed all things according to the Law of the Lord, they returned into Galilee, to their own city Nazareth. And the child grew and waxed strong in spirit, filled with wisdom, and the grace of God was upon him"* (Luke 2: 40). The notable exception was the account of the Passover trip to Jerusalem when Jesus was 12 years old, went missing and was then found by Mary and Joseph in the temple 'about his Father's business' and: *"sitting in the midst of the doctors, both hearing them and asking them questions."*

Thereafter, in the final verses of Luke chapter 2, we again get a short statement from Mary of the childhood years of Jesus from the age of 12: *"And he went down with them, and came to Nazareth, and was subject unto them: and his mother kept all these sayings in her heart. And Jesus advanced in wisdom and stature, and in favor with God and men"* (Luke 2: 51-52).

---

1   See *Joseph's Testament of the First Christmas*, Philip Robinson, (USAP 2021)

In remarkably similar fashion (and beginning with exactly the same words), the final verse of *Luke* chapter 1 provides us with a short summary of the childhood years of John the Baptist, after his circumcision: *"And the child grew and waxed strong in spirit, and was in the desert till the day of his shewing unto Israel"* (Luke 1: 80).

But the years of youth were very different for each. Jesus remained in the family home in Nazareth until his ministry began, while John lived in the wilderness, dressed in *"raiment of camel's hair, and a leathern girdle about his loins; and his meat was locusts and wild honey"* (Matthew 3: 4).

Chapter 9

John the Baptist's wilderness years

Locusts and wild honey

The food that John ate in the wilderness was 'locusts and wild honey', a phrase that has an echo of the Old Testament description of the Promised Land as 'flowing with milk and honey' – clearly not literally, but representing a land rich in pasture (for milk) and arable (for blossoms). The wilderness had no 'pasture' but enough green and flowering vegetation to support locusts and bees.

The angel Gabriel had told Zacharias that John would 'drink no wine or strong drink', but in later years Jesus added to our knowledge of his wilderness diet by telling us that he didn't eat bread either: *"John the Baptist came neither eating bread nor drinking wine"* (Luke 7: 33).

Camel hair and leather belt

The clothing that John wore in the wilderness was *"raiment of camel's hair, and a leathern girdle about his loins"*, a clear echo of the clothing of the Old Testament prophet Elijah, who was *"an hairy man, and girt with a girdle of leather about his loins. And he said, It is Elijah the Tishbite"* (2 Kings 1: 8).

In the spirit and power of Elijah

The angel Gabriel had prophesied to Zacharias that John would *"go before his face in the spirit and power of Elijah, to turn the hearts of the fathers to the children, and the disobedient to walk in the wisdom of the just; to make ready for the Lord a people prepared for him"* (Luke 1: 17). This was a part fulfilment of the Old Testament promise by God to Israel that he would send *"Elijah the prophet before the great and terrible day of Jehovah come. And he shall turn the heart of fathers to the children and the heart of the children to their fathers"* (Malachi 4: 5-6).

It may seem like a semantic difference as to whether John the Baptist had actually 'come back' as the prophet Elijah or only come 'in the spirit or power of Elijah', but it was an important distinction. Until Jesus would be rejected as King in Jerusalem, crucified and resurrected, it was not revealed that the coming of Elijah and the 'great and awesome day of the Lord' – and the millennial kingdom – would be deferred to a second Advent.

So John himself denied he was Elijah, but declared himself as *"the voice of one crying in the wilderness, Make straight the way of the Lord, as said Isaiah the prophet."* (John 1: 23), and Jesus left the distinction blurred for the time being: *"Verily I say unto you, Among them that are born of women there hath not risen a greater than John the Baptist ... And **if ye are willing to receive it, this is Elijah**, that is to come."* (Matthew 11: 11, 14).

Chapter 10

The ministry of John the Baptist – Preparing the Way

The early ministry of John, before his great encounter with the Lord when Jesus came to be baptised, is recorded in each of the four Gospels:

(Matthew 3: 1-12) *"And in those days cometh John the Baptist, preaching in the wilderness of Judaea, saying, Repent ye: for the kingdom of heaven is at hand. For this is he that was spoken of through Isaiah the prophet, saying, The voice of one crying in the wilderness, Make ye ready the way of the Lord, Make his paths straight. Now John himself had his raiment of camel's hair, and a leathern girdle about his loins; and his food was locusts and wild honey.*

Then went out unto him Jerusalem, and all Judaea, and all the region round about the Jordan; and they were baptized of him in the river Jordan, confessing their sins. But when he saw many of the Pharisees and Sadducees coming to his baptism, he said unto them, Ye offspring of vipers, who warned you to flee from the wrath to come? Bring forth therefore fruit worthy of repentance: and think not to say within yourselves, We have Abraham to our father: for I say unto you, that God is able of these stones to raise up children unto Abraham. And even now the axe lieth at the root of the trees: every tree therefore that bringeth not forth good fruit is hewn down, and cast into the fire. I indeed baptize you in water unto repentance. but he that cometh after me is mightier than I, whose shoes I am not worthy to bear: he shall baptize you in the Holy Spirit and in fire: whose fan is in his hand, and he will thoroughly cleanse his threshing-floor, and he will gather his wheat into the garner; but the chaff he will burn up with unquenchable fire."

(Mark 1: 1-8) *"Even as it is written in Isaiah the prophet, Behold, I send my messenger before thy face, who shall prepare thy way. The voice of one crying in the wilderness, Make ye ready the way of the Lord, Make his paths straight.*

John came, who baptized in the wilderness, and preached the baptism of repentance unto remission of sins. And there went out unto him all the country of Judaea, and all they of Jerusalem, and they were baptized of him in the river Jordan, confessing their sins. And John was clothed with camel's hair, and had a leathern girdle about his loins; and did eat locusts and wild honey; And he preached, saying, There cometh after me he that is mightier than I, the latchet of whose shoes I am not worthy to stoop down and unloose. I baptized you in water: but he shall baptize you in the Holy Spirit."

(Luke 3: 1-18) *"Now in the fifteenth year of the reign of Tiberius Caesar, Pontius Pilate being governor of Judaea, and Herod being tetrarch of Galilee, and his brother Philip tetrarch of Ituraea and Trachonitis, and Lysanias the tetrarch of Abilene, in the high-priesthood of Annas and Caiaphas, the word of God came unto John the son of Zacharias in the wilderness.*

And he came into all the region round about the Jordan, preaching the baptism of repentance unto remission of sins; As it is written in the book of the words of Isaiah the prophet, The voice of one crying in the wilderness, Make ye ready the way of the Lord, Make his paths straight. Every valley shall be filled, and every mountain and hill shall be brought low; and the crooked shall become straight, and the rough ways shall be made smooth; And all flesh shall see the salvation of God.

He said therefore to the multitudes that came forth to be baptized of him, Ye offspring of vipers, who warned you to flee from the wrath to come? Bring forth therefore fruits worthy of repentance, and begin not to say within yourselves, We have Abraham to our father: for I say unto you, that God is able of these stones to raise up children unto Abraham. And even now the axe also lieth at the root of the trees: every tree therefore that bringeth not forth good fruit is hewn down, and cast into the fire.

And the multitudes asked him, saying, What then must we do? And he answered and said unto them, He that hath two coats, let him impart to him that hath none; and he that hath food, let him do likewise. And there came also publicans to be baptized, and said unto him, Teacher, what must we do? And he said unto them, Extort no more than that which is appointed you. And soldiers also asked him, saying, And we, what must we do? And he said unto them, Extort from no man by violence, neither accuse any one wrongly; and be content with your wages.

And as the people were in expectation, and all men reasoned in their hearts concerning John, whether he haply were the Christ; John answered, saying unto them all, I indeed bap-tize you with water but there cometh he that is mightier than I, the latchet of whose shoes I am not worthy to unloose: he shall bap-tize you in the Holy Spirit and in fire: whose fan is in his hand, thoroughly to cleanse his threshing-floor, and to gather the wheat into his garner; but the chaff he will burn up with unquenchable fire. With many other exhorta-tions therefore preached he good tidings unto the people."

(John 1: 6-9) *"There came a man, sent from God, whose name was John. The same came for witness, that he might bear witness of the light, that all might believe through him. He was not the light, but came that he might bear witness of the light. There was the true light, even the light which lighteth every man, com-ing into the world."*

(John 1: 19-28) *"And this is the witness of John, when the Jews sent unto him from Je-rusalem priests and Levites to ask him, Who art thou? And he confessed, and denied not; and he confessed, I am not the Christ. And they asked him, What then? Art thou Elijah? And he saith, I am not. Art thou the proph-et? And he answered, No. They said therefore unto him, Who art thou? that we may give an answer to them that sent us.*

What sayest thou of thyself? He said, I am the voice of one crying in the wilderness, Make straight the way of the Lord, as said Isaiah the prophet. And they had been sent from the Pharisees.

And they asked him, and said unto him, Why then baptizest thou, if thou art not the Christ, neither Elijah, neither the prophet? John answered them, saying, I baptize in water: in the midst of you standeth one whom ye know not, even he that cometh after me, the latchet of whose shoe I am not worthy to unloose. These things were done in Bethany beyond the Jordan, where John was baptizing."

The essential ingredients of John's message are repeated by all the Gospel writers: To announce that the kingdom of heaven was at hand; to call for individual confession of sins and repentance; to perform a baptism of repentance with water for the remission of sins; and to warn of the wrath to come for those who didn't live a life displaying 'fruits worthy of repentance'. This meant those that had two coats giving one to those who had none; similarly with food; for tax-collectors to only exact the official rate; and for soldiers to do violence to no man, nor make false accusations, and to be content with their wages.

In establishing the practise of baptism that would be later confirmed as an integral 'church' practice by Jesus, John repeatedly declared although he 'baptised with water', one mightier than him would come who would 'baptise with the Holy Spirit and with fire'.

Remembering that John was a Levite from a priestly parentage, his address to the Sadducees and Pharisees as a 'generation of vipers' fleeing from the wrath to come – and delivered in the wilderness rather than in the temple, was poignant. But it is clear that John fully expected the 'great and awesome' day of judgement where the Messiah would purge with fire the unrepentant self-important religious leaders to be imminent.

Chapter 11

The meeting of Jesus and John the Baptist at the Baptismal Waters

"Then cometh Jesus from Galilee to the Jordan unto John, to be baptized of him. But John would have hindered him, saying, I have need to be baptized of thee, and comest thou to me? But Jesus answering said unto him, Suffer it now: for thus it becometh us to fulfil all righteousness. Then he suffereth him. And Jesus, when he was baptized, went up straightway from the water: and, lo, the heavens were opened unto him, and he saw the Spirit of God descending as a dove, and coming upon him; and lo, a voice out of the heavens, saying, This is my beloved Son, in whom I am well pleased" (Matthew 3: 13-17).

The baptism of Jesus by John in the Jordan marked the approaching fulfilment of John's ministry, and the beginning of the public ministry of Jesus. But it was a pivotal event in the Gospel story in more ways than one.

John had publicly declared before this that he himself was not the Christ, but that *"one mightier than I cometh, the latchet of whose shoes I am not worthy to unloose: he shall baptize you with the Holy Spirit and with fire."* Who was this? John answered that *"there standeth one among you, whom ye know not; He it is, who coming after me is preferred before me."*

When Jesus appeared in front of John to be baptised by him, John at first refused, saying that instead he needed to be baptised by Jesus! But it was to be done this way *"to fulfil all righteousness."* Then, as Jesus came up out of the water, the Trinity manifested together on earth. The Spirit of God descended on Jesus like a dove, and the Father said from heaven: *"This is my beloved Son, in whom I am well pleased."*

Immediately, Jesus was led into the wilderness by the Spirit, fasting for 40 days, to be tempted by Satan.

"On the morrow he seeth Jesus coming unto him, and saith, Behold the Lamb of God, that taketh away the sin of the world. This is he of whom I said, After me cometh a man who is become before me: for he was before me. And I knew him not: but that he should be made manifest to Israel, for this cause came I baptizing in water. And John bare witness, saying, I have beheld the Spirit descending as a dove out of heaven; and it abode upon him. And I knew him not; but he that sent me to baptize in water, he said unto me, Upon whomsoever thou shalt see the Spirit descending, and abiding upon him, the same is he that baptizeth in the Holy Spirit. And I have seen, and have borne witness that this is the Son of God" (John 1: 29-34).

Before Jesus presented himself for baptism, John knew the Messiah he was proclaiming was 'among the people', but hadn't 'shown' himself yet. He says 'I knew him not' but he only knew that he was about to be made 'manifest to Israel', and that God had told John "upon whom thou shalt see the Spirit descending, and abiding on him, the same is he that baptizeth in the Holy Spirit." And John declared to his own disciples, "And I have seen, and have borne witness that this is the Son of God."

Although John did not know Jesus until this point, it is inconceivable that Jesus did not only know who John the Baptist was, as did 'the multitude', but that John's mother and his own mother Mary were 'cousins'. Mary's testament on this would not have been kept from her son. But John, whose elderly parents probably died when he was young, and since had lived alone in the wilderness, had no way of recognising him other than through the sign that God had promised.

Chapter 12

John the Baptist points his own 'prepared' disciples to Jesus

When the Temptation of Jesus by Satan in the wilderness of Judea was over, Jesus returned to the scene of his baptism, and the transition of ministries from John to Jesus was about to be sealed.

> *"On the morrow he seeth Jesus coming unto him, and saith, Behold, the Lamb of God, that taketh away the sin of the world! ... Again on the morrow John was standing, and two of his disciples; and he looked upon Jesus as he walked, and saith, Behold, the Lamb of God! And the two disciples heard him speak, and they followed Jesus"* (John 1: 29, 35-37).

This declaration by John the Baptist to two of his own disciples is of momentous significance. Jesus was being identified by John as the promised Messiah, the 'Son of God', and now also as the 'Lamb of God that taketh away the sins of the world', a new title that identified Jesus with the Passover Lamb that was only a foreshadowing of the final sacrifice at Calvary.

In the popular mind today, the first four disciples of Jesus – Simon Peter and his brother Andrew, and James and John the two sons of Zebedee – were first called from their fishing boats on the shore of Lake Galilee to 'become fishers of men'. But the following verses from the Apostle John's *Gospel* reveal that the 'calling' on the shore was not a first encounter, but a final call for them to 'forsake all' and become full-time followers and apostles.

The two disciples of John the Baptist that had Jesus pointed out to them as the 'Lamb of God' and the 'Son of God' were: Andrew (Peter's younger brother) and John (James's younger brother). This 'other' John (not to be confused with John the Baptist) was the 'beloved disciple' who otherwise remains unnamed throughout his own *Gospel*, and who ultimately receives the vision of the 'Lamb of God' on the throne in his book of *Revelation*.

Having 'followed Jesus' rather than John the Baptist from this point, John and Andrew leave and go with Jesus to the place where he was dwelling. Almost immediately, Andrew brought his brother Simon Peter to Jesus saying "we have found the Messiah", and the gathering of Jesus's first disciples continued apace on their return from Judea to Galilee.

> *"Again on the morrow John was standing, and two of his disciples; and he looked upon Jesus as he walked, and saith, Behold, the Lamb of God! And the two disciples heard him speak, and they followed Jesus. And Jesus turned, and beheld them following, and saith unto them, What seek ye? And they said unto him, Rabbi, (which is to say, being interpreted, Teacher)*

where abidest thou? He saith unto them, Come and ye shall see. They came therefore and saw where he abode, and they abode with him that day: it was about the tenth hour.

One of the two that heard John speak, and followed him, was Andrew, Simon Peter's brother. He findeth first his own brother Simon, and saith unto him, We have found the Messiah, (which is, being interpreted, Christ). He brought him unto Jesus. Jesus looked upon him, and said, Thou art Simon the son of John: thou shalt be called Cephas (which is by interpretation, Peter)." (John 1: 35-42).

Chapter 13

John the Baptist in prison, still pointing his disciples to Jesus

There was not much more than a year, perhaps only months, of an overlap between the two ministries, for shortly after Jesus began his public ministry, John the Baptist was imprisoned by King Herod. But John's disciples were still able to visit him, and they began to question why, if Jesus was about to be crowned 'King of the Jews' in earthly terms, things seemed to be moving in the opposite direction. By sending his disciples to Jesus with a direct question, was John yet again deliberately pointing his disciples to Christ?

> *"Now when John heard in prison the works of the Christ, he sent by his disciples, and said unto him, Art thou he that cometh, or look we for another? And Jesus answered and said unto them, Go and tell John the things which ye hear and see: the blind receive their sight, and the lame walk, the lepers are cleansed, and the deaf hear, and the dead are raised up, and the poor have good tidings preached to them. And blessed is he, whosoever shall find no occasion of stumbling in me.*

And as these went their way, Jesus began to say unto the multitudes concerning John, What went ye out into the wilderness to behold? a reed shaken with the wind? But what went ye out to see? a man clothed in soft raiment? Behold, they that wear soft raiment are in kings' houses. But wherefore went ye out? to see a prophet? Yea, I say unto you, and much more than a prophet. This is he, of whom it is written, Behold, I send my messenger before thy face, Who shall prepare thy way before thee. Verily I say unto you, Among them that are born of women there hath not arisen a greater than John the Baptist: yet he that is but little in the kingdom of heaven is greater than he. And from the days of John the Baptist until now the kingdom of heaven suffereth violence, and men of violence take it by force. For all the prophets and the law prophesied until John. And if ye are willing to receive it, this is Elijah, that is to come" (Matthew 11: 2-14).

So John, from his prison cell, sent two of his disciples to ask Jesus if he was the one "that should come or do we look for another?" Was this an indication that John had himself begun to doubt that Jesus was the Christ? Like the whole nation of Israel, from Herod down to the humblest believer, the promise of a Messiah included the expectation of a new messianic kingdom – with a 'Son of David' on the actual throne of Israel – heralding the 'wrath to come' in a Day of Vengeance. This expectation gave hope to the poor, and triggered hostility in the hearts of those in power.

The surprising answer that Jesus gave to John's disciples was full of oblique meaning: *"Go and shew John again those things which ye do hear and see: The blind receive their sight, and the lame walk, the lepers are cleansed, and the deaf hear, the dead are raised up and the poor have the gospel preached to them."* It was not simply a message that no-one but the Messiah could perform such miracles. These very words echo those that Jesus used (quoting from *Isaiah* 60) right at the start of his public ministry in Nazareth on his return to Galilee after his baptism:

> *"And Jesus returned in the power of the Spirit into Galilee: and a fame went out concerning him through all the region round about. And he taught in their synagogues, being glorified of all. And he came to Nazareth, where he had been brought up: and he entered as his custom was, into the synagogue on the sabbath day, and stood up to read. And there was delivered unto him the book of the prophet Isaiah. And he opened the book, and found the place where it was written,*

> **The Spirit of the Lord is upon me, Because he hath anointed me to preach good tidings to the poor: He hath sent me to proclaim re-**

lease to the captives, And recovering of sight to the blind, To set at liberty them that are bruised, To proclaim the acceptable year of the Lord.

And he closed the book, and he gave it back to the attendant, and sat down: and the eyes of all in the synagogue were fastened on him. And he began to say unto them, To-day hath this scripture been fulfilled in your ears" (Luke 4: 14-21).

When we look closely at what Jesus read on that occasion from *Isaiah* 60, and we discover that in the middle of a sentence he 'closed the book and gave it again to the minister, and sat down'. Then he declared: *"This day is this scripture fulfilled in your ears."*

But it is important to understand what he didn't read as much as what he did. He ended his reading with **"To preach the acceptable year of the Lord ..."** closing the book where the passage continues in the original **"... and the day of vengeance of our God."**

"The Spirit of the Lord Jehovah is upon me; because Jehovah hath anointed me to preach good tidings unto the meek; he hath sent me to bind up the broken-hearted, to proclaim liberty to the captives, and the opening of the prison to them that are bound; to proclaim the year of Jehovah's favor, *and the day* *of vengeance of our God; to comfort all that mourn"* (Isaiah 60: 1-2).

The day of vengeance was not to be fulfilled by Jesus in his first Advent, but after his rejection would await his second coming. This was the message to John the Baptist in prison, and to his remaining disciples. But the reality of two Advents could only unfold as and when Jesus was rejected as King by Israel during his first Advent. In this case of the predestined unfolding of the two Advents of Christ rested on God's foreknowledge of the outcome of his freely offered choice during the first.

EPILOGUE

JOHN THE BAPTIST IS BEHEADED BY HEROD

"At that season Herod the tetrarch heard the report concerning Jesus, and said unto his servants, This is John the Baptist; he is risen from the dead; and therefore do these powers work in him.

For Herod had laid hold on John, and bound him, and put him in prison for the sake of Herodias, his brother Philip's wife. For John said unto him, It is not lawful for thee to have her. And when he would have put him to death, he feared the multitude, because they counted him as a prophet. But when Herod's birthday came, the daughter of Herodias danced in the midst, and pleased Herod. Whereupon he promised with an oath to give her whatsoever she would ask. And she, being put forward by her mother, saith, Give me here on a platter the head of John the Baptist. And the king was grieved; but for the sake of his oaths, and of them that sat at meat with him, he commanded it to be given; and he sent, and beheaded

John in the prison. And his head was brought on a platter, and given to the damsel: and she brought it to her mother. And his disciples came, and took up the corpse, and buried him, and they went and told Jesus. Now when Jesus heard it, he withdrew from thence in a boat, to a desert place apart: and when the multitudes heard thereof, they followed him on foot from the cities" (Matthew 14: 1-13).

This tragic end to John the Baptist's life came before he could witness the completion of Jesus's ministry, crucifixion, resurrection and ascension in the first Advent. It must have sent a traumatic shock wave through the band of Jesus's own followers, not to mention the remaining disciples of John the Baptist, whose first response after burying his body was to go and report it to Jesus.

Just as Jesus's life appeared to end in horrific failure on the cross, but in the resurrection was the ultimate victory over Satan and death itself, so John the Baptist's death also appeared to end in horrific failure. But he had completed his task of 'preparing the way', and died the death of an Old Testament prophet, martyred like so many of the prophets before him by Israel's ungodly leadership.

Jesus's final testimony of John the Baptist declared him the greatest of all the prophets, but told the multitude that the least in the coming kingdom of God would be even greater than him.

"And when the messengers of John were departed, he began to say unto the multitudes concerning John, What went ye out into the wilderness to behold? a reed shaken with the wind? But what went ye out to see? a man clothed in soft raiment? Behold, they that are gorgeously apparelled, and live delicately, are in kings' courts. But what went ye out for to see? a prophet? Yea, I say unto you, and much more than a prophet. This is he of whom it is written, Behold, I send my messenger before thy face, Who shall prepare thy way before thee. I say unto you, Among them that are born of women there is none greater than John: yet he that is but little in the kingdom of God is greater than he.

And all the people when they heard, and the publicans, justified God, being baptized with the baptism of John. But the Pharisees and the lawyers rejected for themselves the counsel of God, being not baptized of him" (Luke 7: 24-30).

As John the Baptist's name suggests, his ministry of preparation involved a baptism of repentance for the remission of sins. Those in the multitude addressed by Jesus *"justified God, being baptized with the baptism of John. But the Pharisees and lawyers rejected the counsel of God against themselves, being not baptized of him."*

John the Baptist's seemingly inglorious end did not mark the demise of a failed prophet, but the perfectly obedient fulfilment of his prophetic role as the last and greatest of the 'Old Testament' martyred prophets and saints – a life led 'in the spirit and power of Elijah'.

POSTSCRIPT

THE BAPTISM OF JOHN IN THE EARLY CHURCH

When Jesus insisted, under protest from John the Baptist, that he himself would be baptised *"to fulfil all righteousness"*, it served as a seal of approval of the practice, and a perfect example for his followers both then and in the future. John, however, had claimed that while he baptised with water, *"he that cometh after me is mightier than I … he shall baptize you with the Holy Spirit, and with fire."*

During the short time that their ministries overlapped, both John and Jesus were baptising, although in Jesus's case it was his disciples rather than the Lord himself performing the baptism:

> *"When therefore the Lord knew that the Pharisees had heard that Jesus was making and baptizing more disciples than John, (**although Jesus himself baptized not, but his disciples**), he left Judaea, and departed again into Galilee"* (John 4: 1-3).

In the 'Great Commission' given by Jesus to his disciples just before his Ascension, baptism was to be an essential part of their mission:

*"And Jesus came to them and spake unto them, saying, All authority hath been given unto me in heaven and on earth. **Go ye therefore, and make disciples of all nations, baptizing them in the name of the Father, and of the Son, and of the Holy Spirit**: teaching them to observe all things whatsoever I commanded you: and, lo, I am with you always, even unto the end of the world"* (Matthew 28: 18-20).

In the *Acts of the Apostles*, there are numerous mentions of baptisms being part and parcel of the life of the early church. But two examples stand out in the context of their reference to 'the baptism of John'.

The first occasion was about 10 years after Jesus's Ascension, in the house of a Roman centurion, a gentile called Cornelius who was stationed in Caesarea. Cornelius was a devout, God-fearing man whose prayers were answered when an angel told him to send to Joppa and call for a man called Simon Peter who *"shall tell thee what thou oughtest to do."* When the Apostle Peter arrived with 'certain brethren', Cornelius said: *"we are all here before God, to hear all things that are commanded thee of God."*

Peter responded:

"Of a truth I perceive that God is no respecter of persons:

*but in every nation that feareth him, and worketh righteousness, is acceptable to him. The word which he sent unto the children of Israel, preaching good tidings of peace by Jesus Christ: (he is Lord of all) – that saying ye yourselves know, which was published throughout all Judaea, beginning from **Galilee, after the baptism which John preached**; even Jesus of Nazareth, how God anointed him with the Holy Spirit and with power: who went about doing good, and healing all that were oppressed of the devil; for God was with him. And we are witnesses of all things which he did both in the country of the Jews, and in Jerusalem; whom also they slew, hanging him on a tree: Him God raised up the third day, and gave him to be made manifest, not to all the people, but unto witnesses that were chosen before of God, even to us, who ate and drank with him after he rose from the dead. And he charged us to preach unto the people, and to testify that this is he who is ordained of God to be the Judge of the living and the dead. To him bear all the prophets witness, that through his name everyone that believeth on him shall receive remission of sins"* (Acts 10: 34- 43)

While Peter was speaking these words, the Holy Spirit fell on all his listeners and Peter's companions were amazed because the Holy Spirit had been poured out on uncircumcised gentiles who spoke in tongues and glorified God.

Then Peter declared with authority:

> *"Can any man forbid the water, that these should not be baptized, who have received the Holy Spirit as well as we? And he commanded them to be baptized in the name of Jesus Christ"* (Acts 10: 47-48).

The water-baptism of John was not necessarily accompanied by the regenerative 'baptism of the Spirit', but it was associated with it – in this case the gift of the Holy Spirit came before baptism.

The second illustration from *Acts of the Apostles* occurred about another 10 years later, in Ephesus, while the Apostle Paul was passing through. Here the sequence of receiving the Holy Spirit first, and then baptism was reversed. Paul had found a group of about a dozen disciples that had received the baptism of John, but they knew nothing of the Holy Spirit:

> *"He said unto them, Did ye receive the Holy Spirit when ye believed? And they said unto him, Nay, we did not so much as hear whether the Holy Spirit was given. And he said, Into what then were ye baptized? And they said, Into John's baptism. And Paul said, John baptized with the baptism of repentance, saying unto the people that they should believe on him that should come after him, that is, on*

Jesus. And when they heard this, they were baptized into the name of the Lord Jesus. And when Paul had laid his hands upon them, the Holy Spirit came on them; and they spake with tongues, and prophesied. And they were in all about twelve men." (Acts 19: 2-7).

John the Baptist's ministry had been one of preparation of the people to receive Christ. He preached a baptism of repentance of sins, and as people repented, they showed their change of heart by an outward cleansing. But for the regeneration of the 'new birth' repentance was not enough. The people must have Christ. They must be 'born' of water *and* the Spirit. As Jesus told the Pharisee, Nicodemus:

*"Verily, verily, I say unto thee, **Except one be born of water and the Spirit, he cannot enter into the kingdom of God**. That which is born of the flesh is flesh; and that which is born of the Spirit is spirit. Marvel not that I said unto thee, Ye must be born anew. The wind bloweth where it will, and thou hearest the voice thereof, but knowest not whence it cometh, and whither it goeth: so is every one that is born of the Spirit"* (John 3: 5-8).